Illusions

MY JOURNEY TO FREEDOM

CORINA TAYLOR

BALBOA.PRESS

A DIVISION OF HAY HOUSE

Balboa Press books may be ordered through booksellers or by contacting:

Balboa Press
A Division of Hay House
1663 Liberty Drive
Bloomington, IN 47403
www.balboapress.com
844-682-1282

Cover artist credit:
Savannah Lockie
Instagram @savannah.lindsay

Print information available on the last page.

ISBN: 978-1-6698-2509-8 (sc)
ISBN: 978-1-6698-2510-4 (e)

Balboa Press rev. date: 12/14/2021

To Anderson and Audrey

And to Bernard Lietaer, you were a visionary. Thank you for your lifetime of work to make this world more equitable, sustainable and kind

UPHEAVAL

To be nobody but yourself in a world which is doing
its best, night and day, to make you everybody
else—means to fight the hardest battle which
any human can fight; and never stop fighting.
—e. e. cummings

I WAS HOLDING MY HUSBAND'S HAND WHEN HE TOOK HIS last breath. I felt a whoosh of energy leave his body and he was gone.

Paul died just a few days after we celebrated his fifty-second birthday. We were in Hawaii with a group of friends, where he was competing in a triathlon. Paul wasn't your typical triathlete. He worked long hours running an investment bank and traveled constantly— both of which contributed to his high blood pressure and cholesterol.

He had signed up for the race to get in shape for our young kids, who were four and six at the time. He was goal oriented, so he needed something to aim for. I suggested he start smaller by joining a gym or going for a regular run on our treadmill. But Paul liked big gestures, and his ego was in play, so a triathlon it was. He hired a trainer and got to work.

The decision turned out to be deadly. He had a heart attack in the water, and it took several minutes to resuscitate him. When the paramedics finally got his heart beating again, he had been without oxygen for over ten minutes.

I was oblivious to all this at the time. The kids and I were at the opposite end of the beach, where the swimmers finish. We waited as the competitors in his age group started to get out of the water. My camera was fixed on the finishers, not wanting to miss the shot. When everyone in Paul's heat was out, we waited some more. But something felt off. Our friend Sarah went to ask an official if they recorded Paul's time in case we somehow missed him. As she walked back, I knew instantly something was wrong.

Paul was being taken by ambulance to the hospital. He had been pulled out of the water early in the swim after suffering a heart attack. I gathered the kids, and we rushed after him. The forty-minute drive felt like a lifetime. My friend Daniel was behind the wheel as I stared at my phone, willing it not to ring. I thought, *If they don't call, he's still alive.* Daniel and I barely spoke. Both of us knew how bad this was. The kids were in the back seat playing I spy and speculating on how many bandages Daddy would need. They were oblivious to the potential of their lives being torn apart.

At the hospital, an MRI showed significant swelling in Paul's brain. Doctors cooled his body and put him in an induced coma to try to reduce the swelling. After a couple of days Paul's organs started to fail, and multiple tests and scans showed no sign of brain activity.

UNRAVELING A LIFE

*… and sometimes you have to die just a little bit
inside before you really understand how to live.*
—Unknown

When I sat down to write Paul's obituary, I wrote the fairy tale. I chose the story where he was the doting husband and father, the successful businessman and generous donor. It was the story I, and most everyone around me, wanted to believe. Death makes people keen to gloss over the rough edges. This was an opportunity to crystalize the good, and I suppose it's human nature to do so when a loved one dies. In a way, it felt not only necessary, but required. I included some highs and lows, but nothing to tarnish the tale. It wasn't untrue, but it was only part of a much larger story.

Six years after that day on the beach in Hawaii, I understand that Paul's death was not the bottom; it was the beginning. The beginning of unravelling and uncovering every uncomfortable truth about myself, my relationships, the world we inhabit, and the systems and structures that silently govern our beliefs and behaviors. Specifically, truths about death, sex, and money. Taboos in our culture that therefore are understood by most in a rudimentary and distorted way. These three things intersect at the most fundamental level and inform almost everything we do in life. And our relationship to them is controlled and centralized in ways that most people can't begin to fathom.

But let me go back.

MASKS AND COPING MECHANISMS

We carry the debt of our ancestors.

—Unknown

I GREW UP IN A SMALL TOWN IN THE INTERIOR OF BRITISH Columbia, Canada. My parents moved there in 1974. They were looking for a perfect place to raise their kids. They wanted to give us the ideal childhood, something they both missed out on.

My mom's dad was a raging alcoholic. Her mother emigrated from Syria as a young child and suffered from depression. It fell on my mom to make sure her dad got home safely from the bars so he didn't lose his driver's license again and therefore his ability to make a living. They lived in Oak Bay, a Waspy neighborhood in Victoria, British Columbia. Their house was rented, which, along with her dad's drinking and mom's darker skin, added to her feeling like an outsider and never good enough. She coped by creating the illusion that everything was perfect.

When we were growing up, Mom got up at 5:45 each morning. Without fail, she did her hair and makeup and dressed like a million dollars to drive to the grocery store or run errands. That was her armor, and it kept her safe.

It still does. Motherhood and PTA meetings were the "desirable" and available destinations after marriage. *Fit the mold and don't question things*, life in a small town in the '70s seemed to say.

My dad's family moved frequently from small town to small town because my grandfather was an RCMP officer. My father's parents split up when he was young. His mother left to pursue a life as a singer in a big band traveling across North America. My dad and his siblings were shipped off to boarding school.

I don't know why Grandpa didn't keep his kids when Nana left. When I did hear stories, all complexity was weeded out. The narrative was that Nana abandoned her three young children. And yes, she did. The fact that she married as a teenager and had those kids before she turned twenty did not seem to be relevant in the retelling of the story. No one seemed to consider that her other option may have been to abandon herself. There was no right answer, just heartbreak, no matter which decision she made.

This about sums up what I know about my parents' childhoods. Difficult things weren't discussed in our household. Past traumas were not to be excavated or examined. They were compartmentalized years ago, and that's where they remained. I don't recall any space or desire to question what makes a life. Nothing to add discomfort to the status quo.

Needless to say, I didn't get a lot of emotional guidance from my parents. While they loved me and my sisters dearly, and sacrificed so much for us, they were products of their environments and had shut down emotionally years ago to protect themselves.

Because I didn't feel comfortable talking to my parents about much, especially relationships, I turned to other sources, like magazines. Toxic ones like *Seventeen* and *Cosmopolitan*, which, remarkably, could be found in our school library. I spent a lot of time doing the quizzes to find out "What kind of girl are you?" and reading articles about "What guys want" or "How to French-kiss."

Like many teenagers, I was unsure who I was meant to be in the world, and my only desire was to fit in. I wanted only to do "it" right, whatever "it" was. I tried on different personas, none of which ever felt right because none of them were me. I never let anyone get too close. I was sure everyone else knew what they were doing, and I didn't want to admit my insecurities and doubts.

I didn't know the purpose of life was to be your authentic self. I had no role models for authenticity, just role models for those playing roles. So, my inner world, with all the answers I would ever need, lay dormant as I continually looked outside myself for guidance.

In my tween and teen years, I was engrossed with book series like *Sweet Dreams* and *Sweet Valley High*. In case you are not familiar with these fine works of literature, this is the summary of *Spotlight on Love*, book fifty-five in the *Sweet Dreams* series: "Callie Lloyd is afraid that the girl who was picked instead of her for the lead in the school musical will also steal her new boyfriend, David Palmer, who is playing the male lead." Girls pitted against girls not only for "jobs" but boys. And this from book eighteen, *Ten-Boy Summer*: "Jill's vacation gets off to a wild start when her best friend, Toni, thinks up a contest—who can be the first to date ten new boys! It seems like a great solution to a boring summer until the girls get into a big fight over one of the boys. Suddenly the friendly competition turns into all-out-war."

In these books and magazines that I was inadvertently using as my guideposts, men were one dimensional and relationships a game. As if you can somehow "win" in a relationship. They glorified the chase, and if you succeeded, you were worthy. As far as my teenage self could ascertain, my value was directly linked to the attention I received from boys.

I was competitive and wanted to win at the game. And I became quite good at it. But winning the game wasn't about building a strong relationship. It certainly wasn't about being seen or understood. Honesty and transparency weren't part of the game. Nor was getting my needs met. But I didn't understand that at the time.

Fast-forward thirty years, and I realized I've been playing a version of the game since I was a teenager.

SEEKING MEANING

Not all those who wander are lost.
—J. R. R. Tolkien

Travelling—it gives you a home in a thousand strange places, then leaves you a stranger in your own land.
—Ibn Battuta

I SPENT A CHUNK OF MY MID TO LATE 20s BACKPACKING around Asia, South America, and Africa. I knew there was more to life than what was offered up to that point. It didn't make sense that life was just some combination of work, exercise, shopping, dinner with friends, rinse and repeat. Traveling felt more right than anything I've ever done.

It opened up something in me. I felt freedom for the first time in my life. Freedom from routine, schedules, expectations, paradigms, roles ... everything I didn't realize sucked the life out of life. I got to discard all my masks and exist from a more authentic place. Now, of course, the programming doesn't just dissolve, but it did ease off. And the more I was on the road, the more it faded into the background. I hitchhiked through Lesotho,

Mozambique, Botswana, Namibia, Zambia, and Tanzania. I spent days in a dugout on the Amazon River in Bolivia, I trekked in Patagonia, did an Ayurvedic retreat in Nepal, and vipassana meditation near Dharamshala, India.

I traveled solo for weeks at a time. I would meet up with people here and there, but mostly I was alone. I never felt lonely. I started writing in a journal, trying to make sense of life. It was the start of self discovery. For the first time in twenty-six years, I had the space to contemplate life.

I stayed away as long as I could. But eventually the money ran out and the expectations crept back in. House. Job. Partner. Kids.

At this point, most of my friends were married with children. Only a few of them were particularly happy, yet they were all keen for me to follow their path. It was as if there was only one direction and it was right for everyone. It felt to me that my lifestyle was a direct threat to the decisions they had made. I saw the fear in my girlfriend's eyes as they counseled me not to be so picky with men. Not being pared up felt like a referendum on my character. And at that time, I cared deeply about people's reaction to me. I believed it was my job to make them comfortable. I began to question my newly awakened knowing. And I got sucked back into the vortex.

Shoulds were everywhere—"you should get married." As was fear—"you don't want to wait much longer to have kids." I don't remember anyone asking me what my ideal life looked like, nor did I contemplate it deeply myself. There was just an overriding assumption that marriage and kids were the goal. I never questioned the root of that assumption. All "easy" roads seemed to lead in that direction. But often the easy road can also be the one you choose out of fear. Fear of being different, fear of the unknown.

It was under this backdrop that Paul entered my life. I was thirty-two years old. He pursued me from the day we met. He was living in London, England, but was visiting Vancouver, where I was living, for a meeting. He was going through a divorce after being married at twenty-two years old. He didn't know how to be alone, nor did he have any desire to be. I thought I could heal his wounds. That thinking, I now know, was part of my wounding. It made me feel needed and gave me a sense of control which made me feel safe.

It was flattering to have such attention lavished on me. He pulled out all the stops. We went to Thailand, London, Montreal, Paris, and Italy in just the first few months of our relationship. He proposed in Portofino five months after we met. We celebrated on a chartered boat through the Mediterranean. It looked like what books and movies tell us love looks like. It felt exciting and full of possibility. He wasn't the safe choice, but I felt alive. I put aside any doubts I had, the inconvenient questions that might make me reconsider. I shut down my knowing and listened to the shoulds.

This is hard to admit, but I felt a sense of dignity in being chosen. It activated the old patterns in me. Because, despite my love of freedom, I also continued to elevate the need for society's approval above my own desires. I attracted someone based on my wounds, not my wholeness. So did he.

I quit my job as a writer and producer at the Canadian

Broadcasting Corporation and became a wife and mother. Both positions that are glorified in our society until you hold them. I quickly realized there aren't enough "motherhood is the most important job in the world," comments to conceal the inequities in the trade-off.

ROLES, BOXES, CAGES

*All the world's a stage, and all the men
and women merely players; They have
their exits and their entrances, And one
man in his time plays many parts ...*
—William Shakespeare

*How we spend our days is, of course,
how we spend our lives.*
—Annie Dillard

I TOOK ON MY "ROLE" AND POURED MYSELF INTO BEING A mom and wife. I learned to cook and joined a mom's group. I spent countless hours pushing a swing and playing peek-a-boo. I made friends in our new city of Toronto. We hosted dinner parties and playdates. I had everything I thought I wanted, yet I was miserable.

In many ways marriage felt like the end, not the beginning. Our relationship became a static entity with defined roles, rules and expectations, both our own and societies. But gender roles are limiting to both men and women. And once you're in the box, it's very easy to believe you are trapped.

Paul felt safe with me firmly planted in my role of tending to the kids and making dinner. I kept telling myself to be happy. After all I "had it all." Except I didn't, because boxes don't leave much room for growth or expansion.

I craved a deeper connection, especially once the kids came, but at the same time didn't know how to create it. Paul was not emotionally available. He was wounded as a child and had never dealt with his pain. So it came out sideways. Neither of us understood this at the time. He was holding a lot of secrets. And the secrets haunted him. He created his own prison. But he wasn't prepared to be honest with himself or me, so he remained there until he died.

The longer he held his secrets the further apart we drifted, because there is no true intimacy or connection without honesty. Eventually the distance between us felt unbridgeable. And neither of us had the tools we needed to bridge the void. So, while our relationship was loving, it never got much below the surface level.

I wrongly assumed emotional maturity came with age. But maturity is not something that happens spontaneously when you buy a house and have kids. It's a conscious process you have to cultivate. To mature we must look at our shadow. The parts of us that we keep buried away because they seem too painful or shameful to see.

DAMAGE CONTROL

We don't see things as they are,
we see them as we are.
—Anais Nin

We humanize what is going on in the world and
in ourselves only by speaking of it, and in the
course of speaking of it we learn to be human.
—Hannah Arendt

AUDREY WAS BORN TWO MONTHS AFTER WE MOVED TO Toronto. A few weeks after I was home from the hospital, I found a text message on Paul's phone from another woman. He denied cheating, but I knew the truth in my bones. With two kids under two, I had a horrible decision to make, do I leave or stay?

This might seem like a straightforward decision depending on your values, but it felt more like a complex calculation. One I never thought I would have to make. I was very invested in our relationship on many levels. A story had built up around it that suited my ego, my need for security and our place in the community. This was not an honest story by any measure. It was based on what I

17

wanted to see and what I let others see. But nevertheless, it existed, and it was powerful.

Layered on that, deep down I knew Paul loved me, he just didn't know how to love. His needs were not met as a child, so love to him felt like external validation. He craved it. It drove him to succeed at work and it drove his personal life. The more his ego was fed the hungrier it got. No amount of success, money, or status was sufficient to fill his void.

Because of our core wounds, most people on a subconscious level are behaving in ways to get recognition, love, attention or validation from our mom, dad, a grandparent, sibling, or partner. Until you uncover those wounds and heal them, they will control you. And your relationships will play out from your wounded self, not your authentic one.

My wounded self wanted to save Paul. But I learned a hard lesson—you can't do someone's work for them.

I stayed with Paul mostly because I didn't feel strong enough to leave. Other's perception of my life being perfect was more important to me than the truth. On top of that, I had two small kids and hadn't worked in a couple of years. I felt totally disconnected and so far removed from the working world. The on-ramp back in felt inaccessible. I wished I had never given up that side of myself and it felt gone forever.

I don't know that there was a right answer. Staying didn't feel right, but it also felt necessary. So, I buried the truth and the lie lodged in my body. But lies are not benign, they are corrosive.

From the outside you never would have known we

had issues. We mostly carried on as we always had. And I had to live with the uncomfortable truth that I made compromises I never dreamed I would make. Paul no longer felt safe to me.

I felt shame around Paul's cheating. It felt so cliché and common. I also felt shame around deciding to stay. None of this was part of my script. I considered myself a strong woman, but over the years I realized I traded that strength and independence for the material comfort and perceived safety of a marriage. I put all my chips in someone else's basket. The known felt safer than the unknown, no matter how unfulfilling it was. How did I reach the point where I would accept so little?

Laying in bed at night, often seething with resentment towards Paul, I'd find myself looking at him and wonder who he was deep down. I had no idea what was inside him. Neither did he. I'd wonder too who I was and what my hopes and dreams were. I didn't know the answers and had no clue how to access that knowing. I guess that's part of how we got here.

It's very easy to stay in that spot of limbo, to go through the motions of life. And we did for a long time. In that space, it's easy to blame others for your unhappiness. If only he was like this, if only he did that. But I had choices each step of the way.

As I write this, I am omitting so many parts of our life. This is on purpose. Because while this is my story, it is also so many others. This story is universal as the patterns are archetypal.

This script plays out in countless ways, in countless cities around the world everyday.

To be clear, there was no villain or victim in this relationship, no right or wrong, good or bad. Paul was not one dimensional and neither am I, though sometimes the boxes made us behave like we were. There was love and laughter along with pain, frustration, and heartache. Ultimately, it was what it was and with six years of distance I can look at it and see clearly that it didn't happen to me, it happened for me.

Since Paul's death, I have spent a lot of time trying to understand the dynamics of marriage. Why was I so attached to a story that I clung to it even when it no longer served me? *Especially* when it no longer served me. This attachment felt larger than me. It felt like it was coming from outside of me … and it turns out it was.

FEAR

We are not makers of history. We are made by history.
—Martin Luther King, Jr.

WHEN I TRY AND PINPOINT MY PRIMARY EMOTIONS OF that time and even years before, I think of fear. Fear of scarcity, fear of judgment, fear of not being enough. Fear is everywhere we turn; it is the biggest collective emotion on the planet right now. And fear keeps us stuck. It makes us believe we are powerless. Fear will tell you to stay in an unfulfilling marriage, to stick it out in the job that is soul crushing because "it could be worse." Fear will tell you change is scary or bad. Fear will tell you people from other countries, races, or gender orientations don't share your humanity. Fear will convince you "safety" is more important than freedom. Fear will tell you the known is better than the unknown. And fear will sap your energy leading you down the path of least resistance, rather than the path of most fulfillment.

So where did all this fear come from and how did it become so prevalent? Well, it's not an accident. It turns out that fear is baked into a system we use multiple times a day— the monetary system. And the values and emotions inherent in our monetary system are unconsciously activated in every exchange we have. This, of course, has profound repercussions in every aspect of our lives.[1]

I recently stumbled upon a twenty-year-old book by Bernard Lietaer called *The Mystery of Money*. Lietaer was a university professor, Belgian Central Bank executive, and one of the architects of the European Single Currency. He studied monetary systems for over forty years.

Unlike many economists, Lietaer does not believe money is neutral. He says money has been programming our collective unconscious with two primary emotions—greed and scarcity—for thousands of years. Both emotions are linked by fear. These emotions have become so universal, individually and collectively, that we assume they are a natural reaction to money. They are not. They are the result of the values of permanent growth, competition and currency accumulation embedded in our monetary system.[2]

Historically this was not always the case. Some older societies Lietaer studied actively discouraged accumulation of money by valuing sustainability, long term investments and community. This changed the mindset of communities and resulted in a healthier and more balanced societal dynamic.[3]

Our continual use of a system repeats the ideas and emotions of that system. This is how systems maintain themselves. We reinforce them to the point we no longer

---

[1] Bernard Lietaer, *The Mystery of Money* (2000), 82, 228.

[2] Lietaer, 82-86.

[3] Lietaer, 86.

believe we have an option. The system becomes a fact, not a choice.[4]

Every system works this way—medical, educational, political, agricultural, military, etc., and everything is interconnected so the values of one system pervade and activate the others.

---

[4] Lietaer, 228.

OUR MONEY IS OUR POISON

Money is to a civilization as the DNA code is to a species. It replicates structures and behavior patterns that remain active across time and space for generations. It informs billions of individual and collective decisions, big and small ... everyday.
—Bernard Lietaer

Money does not represent such a value as men have placed upon it.
—Nikola Tesla

THIS IS CRUCIALLY IMPORTANT BECAUSE IT'S OUR VERY systems that are causing our demise, propelling us to behave in ways counter to our well-being and often counter to what we truly value. And even if we as individuals don't buy into the values of the system, we end up having to behave in ways that reinforce these values in order to earn money to survive.[5]

This has led to an unbalanced society. And when we are out of balance nothing thrives.

---

[5] Lietaer, 228.

You just need to look around to see that not many people are truly thriving—women or men. Rates of depression, obesity, and suicide are through the roof. Over 70 percent of American adults are on a prescription medication. And I could go on, but I don't need to, as you are living it. This is not the picture of a society that is healthy, physically, or emotionally.

The planet is sick too. We've destroyed much of what sustains us. Our way of life is causing deforestation, biodiversity loss, and pollution on a scale that is inconceivable.

To be clear, money is not the only cause of these problems, but it is certainly a big part of the equation. And society, like individuals, can't heal unless we look clearly at our wounds.

This was starting to make sense to me. But there were still missing pieces. Why, when patriarchy so clearly benefits men, are so many men suffering? Why, in a system that "serves" them in so many ways, are they more likely than women to overdose, spend time in prison, and commit suicide?

It turns out men, like women, have been cut off from their wholeness by the very system they designed. You see there is a divine masculine and a patriarchal masculine, just as there is a divine feminine and a patriarchal feminine. They are entirely different things with entirely different outcomes for individuals and societies.

A NECESSARY BALANCE

Life is a balance of opposites. To deny
one part is to deny your true Self.
—Unknown

FOR THOUSANDS OF YEARS NOW, MASCULINE VALUES HAVE
dominated our ways of being. This has distorted the
masculine and feminine by narrowly defining what a male
looks and acts like, and what a female looks and acts like. It
leaves no room for anyone outside of these narrow boxes.
This has caused devastating wounding, and because of this
the patriarchal male has rejected his feminine energy the
same way society has destroyed the idea of the feminine.

It's helpful to look at it through the lens of the Taoist
concept of Yin Yang. In Taoism everything is energy,
physics will tell you the same thing. Emotions, thoughts,
values, and even systems and structures are all made of
energy. The quality of the energy is either Yin or Yang.
Yin is feminine and Yang masculine. This is not referring
to gender. Each person has both masculine and feminine
energies and balancing the seemingly opposing forces is what
creates equilibrium and a healthy individual and society.
For instance, giving is Yang, receiving is Yin. Activity is

Yang and rest is Yin. Order is Yang and chaos is Yin. The opposing energies are not competing with each other for dominance. They are necessary parts to a whole. The goal is to transcend the opposites and find the middle path.

For example, we don't want to live with 100 percent order because that would look like totalitarianism, if we live with 100 percent chaos that would be dysfunctional and unsustainable. Likewise, if we were constantly active, we would exhaust ourselves. Yet if we were constantly at rest, we would become lazy and impotent. You can see each side is necessary for a balanced individual or culture.

For a person to be emotionally healthy, they need to recognize that they are each made up of masculine and feminine energies. Then then must learn to honor and integrate the different energies. Of course, the balance will look different for everyone.

Below are some masculine or Yang energies and their balancing Yin or feminine energies:

Masculine Energies:	Feminine Energies:
Logical	Intuitive
Assertive	Creative
Focused	Patient
Firm	Gentle
Achieving	Experiencing
Competitive	Collaborative

When energies are out of balance, they manifest like this:

Masculine:	Feminine:
Aggressive	Controlling
Confrontational	Critical
Controlling	Demanding
Critical	Manipulative
Unstable	Over-giving
Unsupportive	People pleasing

When a male succeeds in balancing his energies, he is whole.[6] Externally that looks like a man that is focused and has a purpose. He's logical, nonjudgmental, has integrity and confidence. He embraces his feelings, is humble and honors the feminine.

A female who has balanced her energies honors her truth, knows her worth, and sets healthy boundaries. She is creative, compassionate, and authentic, she asks for what she needs, and she encourages other women to rise with her.

On the other hand, the patriarchal or wounded male normalizes violence and aggression. He is competitive and seeks to control and dominate others, especially women. He thinks vulnerability is a weakness, and disconnects through the intellect, alcohol, food, drugs, video games, or pornography.

The patriarchal or wounded female feels unworthy, is afraid to speak her truth, seeks external validation, overnurtures, overshares, is manipulative, and sees other women as a threat.

---

[6] Lietaer, 75.

My energy became massively imbalanced as soon as I stopped working and no longer had a creative outlet. As much as I wanted to resist the stereotypical role of wife, the paradigm of marriage is a powerful energy. Society aided and abetted that paradigm, taking every opportunity to hoist it on me. I soon felt like a chattel rather than an a capable equal. Most married women I know feel the same. To rebalance the equation, I would try various means to take back some control. For instance, excessively controlling the few things still within my purview, like our dinner plans or where we vacationed. I observed other women become excessive naggers. They would find fault in everything their husband did, never satisfied with any effort. Sometimes women become meek and afraid to voice their opinion. A similar dynamic played out with men who were stay at home dad's or whose spouse was the primary breadwinner. Underneath the nagging, control or subservience was the wounded feminine or wounded masculine—limited by the boxes, roles, and expectations and therefore unable to reach their full potential. So perhaps next time you see a women nagging, controlling, or powerless, rather than judge her, understand underneath that behaviour is probably a lot of buried pain, frustration or anger. She's not a bitch. She's not a doormat. She's wounded.

The wounded masculine and feminine operate from the shadow, a place of insecurity and fear. The unhealthy masculine feeds the unhealthy feminine causing a codependent and cyclical relationship. So, the wounded masculine and feminine reinforce each other the same way systems do.

STEPPING INTO OUR POWER

*And one day she discovered that she was
fierce and strong, and full of fire, and that not
even she could hold herself back because her
passion burned brighter than her fears.*
—Mark Anthony

*She would rather walk alone in darkness
than follow anyone else's shadow.*
—R. G. Moon

So how did patriarchy and the monetary system
combine to bring us to the moment we are in now?

Lietaer traces our current money system back
thousands of years. It was devised at the time patriarchal
societies were overtaking matrifocal societies as the
dominant organizing structure. A matrifocal society
is one where the feminine archetype is honored in the
system equally to men.[7]

As the patriarchy was wiping out more traditional
societies and Judeo-Christian religions becoming

---

[7] Lietaer, 53.

widespread, the patriarchy and church buried a powerful archetype on which matrifocal societies and their monetary systems were structured—The Great Mother/Goddess. And they placed a male god at the center of all things.

An archetype is something we construct our identities around. They represent patterns of behavior that are universally understood at an unconscious level and significantly shape our internal and external realities. Think the hero, villain, teacher, victim, jester, explorer, warrior, child. According to Jung we inherit ideas, emotions, and imagery that inform and motivate how we behave and what we identify with. This is our collective unconscious. Archetypes are so powerful at transmitting ideas and emotions they were used in myths, by Shakespeare, and now in Hollywood movies and advertising.

The Great Mother/Goddess archetype is Mother Earth herself. She encompasses all the natural world—the rocks, trees, plants, and animals. She is the creator of all things.[8] She is the giver of all life and the taker of it. She nurtures and devours. She is mysterious, wise, creative and passionate. She gives abundance and takes it. She asks we meet her wildness with our own, calling forth from us a personal defense of our lives through joyful, passionate, wholehearted living.[9]

When the Great Mother/Goddess archetype was buried, women lost their beacon, their North Star. And

---

[8] Lietaer, 35.

[9] Madronna Holden, *Folklore Lecture Five: Archetypes and the Great Mother*, www.holdenma.wordpress.

men and society lost too. When you honor something, you simultaneously empower it. Of course, the reverse is also true. The powerful divine feminine energy and rightful partner to the divine masculine energy, the energy necessary to bring everything into balance, went underground.

Systems and structures have been designed with almost exclusively Yang energy and values ever since.

With the Great Mother/Goddess pushed to the side, for thousands of years now the feminine has had no representation in the divine. Gods have been exclusively the domain of men. So have the hero archetypes for that matter (with a few exceptions).

The repercussions of this are immense. The Great Mother/Goddess became "sequestered to servile domesticity. ...The woman who was the inspirer becomes the temptress, she who made all things, gods and mortals alike, becomes their plaything, their slave, dowered only with physical beauty."[10] Psychologically women have suffered a "feminine equivalent to male castration" for thousands of years.[11] The divine feminine became the wounded feminine and in turn the divine masculine the wounded masculine. Women no longer had something to live up to, strive for, feel proud of, and empowered by.

When I learned about the Great Mother/Goddess I knew immediately why I felt so numb when I was pushing my kids on the swing or playing hide-and-seek

---

[10] Jane Ellen Harrison, *Prolegomena to The Study of Greek Religion* (Princeton University Press, 1908), 285.

[11] Madronna Holden, *Folklore Lecture Five: Archetypes and the Great Mother*, www.holdenma.wordpress.

day after day. Motherhood was only supposed to be one part of me. It was never meant to be all of me. I was living the wounded feminine. My wildness, passion, and independence had been buried.

If you doubt whether myths or archetypes have power, look at the Christian origin story of Adam and Eve. As the bible tells it, Eve caused the downfall of man with her curiosity. The inherent message for women is follow rules and stay in your lane. Women play no prominent role in the bible. Mary Madeleine, a powerful alchemist in her own right and partner to Jesus, is written off in scripture as a prostitute. Even Mary, the mother of Jesus, is barely mentioned as more than a secondary character. The Christian and patriarchal narrative is that women and evil are intertwined. They need to be tamed and guarded against. Stories build on stories. Layer after layer. And for thousands of years women have had to live within the backdrop of these narratives, trying heroically to overcome them. We have had to operate within the confines of structures that do not represent us, respect us, or value what we value.

Yet now it is so abundantly clear, that it is Eve's very act of curiosity and questioning of authority that will save us and our planet. For she was never our shame to be carried, but our lighthouse in the storm. Our answer was in plain sight for all these years. What if all our answers are staring us in the face? Just waiting for our change in perspective so we can finally see them?

SHADOWS

When an inner situation is not made consciousness, it appears outside of you as fate.

—Carl Jung

Man becomes whole, integrated, calm, fertile, and happy when ... the conscious and the unconscious have learned to live at peace and to complement one another.

—Carl Jung

OVER A PERIOD OF A COUPLE OF HUNDRED YEARS, THE Great Mother/Goddess was pushed from the forefront of our individual and collective psyche to the shadows. It has remained repressed for almost five thousand years. Because we have had no archetype to hold this powerful energy our collective unconscious projects it outward. So, the battles we are fighting externally are really a projection of the ones we don't have the capacity to fight internally. As within, so without.

Lietaer went hunting for the Great Mother/Goddess shadow in the collective unconscious of today's culture to understand it's influence individually and collectively on our lives. And he didn't have to look far.

As we know, when we repress an archetype, all it stands for is distorted. It becomes our shadow. Everything we are told is bad by society, forms our shadow. Our conscious mind rejects it and pushes it deep into our unconscious. Not surprisingly, the three primary attributes of the Great Mother/Goddess are sex, death, and money and the primary shadows are greed and scarcity. And those shadows are so entrenched in our day to day lives that are considered normal.[12]

In today's world, death has become something to guard against rather than a natural form of regeneration. When we repress passion, sex becomes shameful or taboo. We end up trying to legislate what women can do with their bodies and impose puritanical values on their behavior. When we repress the fierceness and wild, we reject intuition and revert to control. We learn only to think, not feel. We become detached from our very essence. Instead of honoring the intelligence and supportive role of the natural world, we try to tame it. When we reject mystery, everything becomes an "other" or a "threat" rather than interconnected. Instead of honoring and stewarding the earth (the Great Mother/Goddess herself), we rape and pillage the land with abandon and with no consideration for all the forms of life that sustain us. Future generations needs are not considered. Everything is about the now and what we can consume, build, control, and overcome.

---

[12] Lietaer, 69–70.

FROM I TO WE

Money often costs too much.
—Ralph Waldo Emerson

The stock market is filled with individuals who know the price for everything, but the value of nothing.
—Phillip Fisher

LET'S GET BACK TO MONEY FOR A MOMENT. NOW THE matrifocal societies Lietaer studied were by no means perfect, but they generally coincided with times of prosperity for all. The divide between peasants and nobleman was relatively small. Working hours were limited. And interestingly, Lietaer found that matrifocal societies had two money systems in place, each with a different purpose.[13]

One was a fiat currency like we have now. It was used only in select interactions that were generally cross border or major purchases. It was centralized by a government or king and prioritized masculine or Yang principles of competition, continual growth, and consumption.

---

[13] Lietaer, 144, 148.

Because the system provides an incentive to save money by paying interest, it is creating and reinforcing greed and scarcity. It punishes those who don't play the game through bankruptcy and poverty. The psychological results of this system are individualism, power concentration, and conquest.[14]

The other money system is called a complementary currency which is devised by the community. It was based on feminine or Yin principles and promoted sustainable abundance, mutual trust, and cooperation. This system encouraged exchanges rather than hoarding by attaching a cost for holding the money for long periods of time. This created a constant flow of money and also encouraged people to think longer term. So rather than holding onto money, people invested it in long term projects like irrigation improvements, textile looms, windmills, or cattle that would create value in the future. The psychological results of this were stronger communities and greater group decision-making. This Yin currency balanced the Yang currency.[15]

But when the matrifocal societies were wiped out, so were the balancing complementary currency systems. We were left with only the Yang system.

Money monopolies, like monocultures, are not healthy or stable. The IMF has counted 145 banking system crashes since 1970 and 72 sovereign debt crashes in the last forty years. None of these happened in Switzerland which has a very stable economy precisely because they

---

[14] Lietaer, 70, 85–86.
[15] Lietaer, 144, 189.

have a complementary currency system in place.[16] The WIR, which was created eighty years ago, is a not-for-profit system. WIR in German means "we," a reminder to members that the economic circle is also a community. It is primarily business to business and over 25 percent of Swiss companies use it. It bypasses banks and doesn't pay interest. It is an electronic debit–credit system that helps business through up and down business cycles, it keeps money circulating and has zero cost to its participants. When it started it had just over a dozen members, there are now over 60,000.

Today there over 5,000 complementary systems in place throughout the world. In Japan there are over 400 systems in place to care for the elderly that don't involve the government. Under one system, if I do something for an elderly person that's not covered by the national health system, say grocery shopping or cooking, I would get a ticket. I can then send that ticket through a clearing house to my elderly mom in another part of the country. She can use it to have someone clean her home, take her for a walk, or any number of things. One hour of service earns one ticket.

In the Berkshire region of Massachusetts, they have created the "BerkShares," a local currency for the region that's accepted at over 400 stores. Using BerkShares encourages money to remain in the region. Doing so benefits not only the stores you're buying from but the wider community, as locally owned businesses tend to source more locally, keep their profits local, and of course pay taxes locally. The people who use this currency make

---

[16] Bernard Lietaer, TEDx Talks, Berlin, November 30, 2009.

a conscious decision to support their community and help foster its independence, sustainability, and well-being.

These types of complementary systems can be created for any type of social purpose like keeping neighborhoods clean, maintaining community gardens, elder care, child care, and environmental action.

We have the ability and technology to tailor systems based on our true values to work alongside our current system. These systems work to keep the "currency" flowing and provide people who are effectively left out of the Yang system ample opportunities to participate and increase their quality of life. They can be structured any number of ways and tailored to the wants, needs, and values of each particular city, province, or country.

CONNECTING OUR STORIES

Evil must disguise itself as good.
—Thomas Aquinas

The devil's job is to look very moral. It has to look like we are defending some great purpose or cause, like 'making the world safe for democracy' or 'keeping the bad people off the street.' Then you can do many evils without any guilt, without any shame or self-doubt, but actually with a sense of high-minded virtue.
—Richard Rohr

WE NOW KNOW THE ARCHETYPAL CHANGES AND THE monetary changes combined to bring us to the inflection point we are facing today.

We also know what the monetary system looks like when its values are out of balance. There are repercussions for all society, individually and collectively. These one-sided values infect and corrupt us all to differing degrees. If there are corrupt individuals— and there are— there are corrupt systems. It's that simple. Systems that most of us take for granted as looking out for our best interest are actually at the mercy of our wounds.

Often the inequities and dysfunction are told in the small stories. The everyday injustices that are almost imperceptible or so commonplace we have come to accept them as unavoidable. That tricks us into not speaking up. Hannah Arendt called this the "banality of evil." We often think that bad or wrongdoing must be dramatic or immediately identifiable as evil in order to be destructive. I remember when "Me Too" began and women started speaking out who had kept quiet for years. I too had experiences with sexual harassment, but in isolation they didn't seem monumental enough to speak up. Like most women, I didn't realize my experiences connected to other women's experience and collectively they added up to a massive tsunami of abuse that women (and in some instances men) have been subjected to in every industry and workplace globally on a daily basis.

Let's not turn a blind eye to the stories, big and small, that can be told from our experiences with every system and structure that was built around a dysfunctional belief system. For if the foundation is rotten, it compromises everything.

It's time we are brave enough to look clearly at our wounds and the relationship between the parts. The aim of therapy is to acknowledge the darkness and bring it into the light to heal it. Collectively our voices are strong. More and more people are starting to speak out and beginning to recognize the injustices and dysfunction embedded in our systems. We are buoyed by the voices that came before us. This is a snowball that can't be stopped. And our voices and values are the solution. We must understand our stories are not shameful, they are liberating.

I have gathered some observations of different systems I have been navigating. The stories below speak to how much of our everyday lives serve to reinforce the status quo, uphold patriarchal values or add to the dysfunction. If you scratch the surface just a little bit, it is clear our systems are not neutral and that we are intellectually and emotionally controlled by them. But once we see our systems clearly, they lose control over us. We get to decide how we interact with them.

I know my stories will connect to your stories to give us a clearer picture of the whole. Let's no longer reverse engineer ourselves to fit these old and crumbling systems. Let's birth a new story, based on our true values that heals, uplifts, and includes us all.

CAPITALISM AS A VALUE

All the money you made will
never buy back your soul.
—Bob Dylan

The oppressors do not perceive their monopoly on
having more as a privilege which dehumanizes
others and themselves. They cannot see that,
in the egoistic pursuit of having as a possessing
class, they suffocate in their own possessions
and no longer are; they merely have.
—Paulo Freire

I WENT TO MANY EVENTS WITH MY HUSBAND— GALAS, cocktail parties, dinner parties. Wherever we were, people wanted his perspective on pretty much anything, regardless of whether he had any experience or background with this particular issue. It became clear, there is a belief that if you're successful in business your opinions on other topics are more valid or valuable than someone else's. Society has crowned businessmen (they are still mostly men) as thought leaders on just about everything. They are the hero's of our capitalist narrative. Their influence is expanded by this elevation in status and we look to them for ideas on how to structure society, even though many of them may never have taken a psychology, ethics, anthropology, or social justice class. And despite the fact that once they reach a certain level of success they are so far removed from the realities of the working class. They live in bubbles that distort their perception and leave their values unchallenged. Most look solely through the lens of capitalism to solve all issues, including social ones like homelessness or the refugee crisis. They truly believe what is right for business is right for society. Capitalism to them is a value and poverty is a character flaw rather than a structural one.

TOXIC MASCULINITY

*The masculinity that's being sold ... is unattainable.
Humans are not intended to suppress their
emotions indefinitely, to always be confident
and unflinching. Traditional masculinity, as
we know it, is an unnatural state, and as a
consequence, men are constantly at war with
themselves and the world around them.*

—Jared Yates Sexton

TODAY'S MALE IS IN A BIND. WE HAVE SO NARROWLY
defined what it is to be male there is little room for men
or boys to feel the full range of human emotions. Be
tough, suck it up, don't cry, be a man, I still hear all the
time. When Paul died, a male relative said to Anderson,
"you're the man of the house now." Anderson was six. I
immediately responded "No, you're not. You're a child,
nothing changes for you." But words can't be unheard.
And with that one sentence, he hoisted upon Anderson
expectations so unattainable and destructive and upon me
so patriarchal and disempowering. Yet it perfectly captures
the battle each gender is fighting for their wholeness and
freedom.

When Kamala Harris was chosen as Joe Biden's running mate there was a lot of talk about firsts. If elected she would be the first female vice president, first black and south Asian vice president. Of course, this potentially and then eventually made her husband the first "second gentlemen." The commentary surrounding this was infuriating. I heard numerous male anchors on network and cable news questioning what he should be called. They chuckled when they said "second gentlemen" as if it wasn't "manly" enough. They proposed "second dude," which seemed more palatable to them. Their tone seemed to imply the job was not serious or substantial enough for a man. In fact, was it even a job when a man held it? Afterall, it's only women in society that are expected to work for free. Toiling away disproportionally at housework, childcare, PTA meetings, and school bake sales, and this is institutionalized in the highest offices (or office adjacent) in the United States as first and second lady, which up until 2021 was always a women working for zero remuneration.

When I tuned into the coverage on inauguration day, anchors were having the same inane "what do we call him" conversation. I never heard anyone suggesting in 2008, Dr. Jill Biden be called Second Chick or Dudette. Not for a second did anyone query whether "second lady" was a substantial enough title or position for DR. JILL BIDEN. DR. There's a sleight of hand in society where we pretend to honor women's contributions, especially if they are of the "right" kind, namely supporting their husbands or raising children. But at the same time, we sideline them through policy and patriarchy. I wonder how many men would willingly switch places with women and be subjected to the same rules and roadblocks? Not the anchors on CNN or MSNBC surely, it was clear they recognized the emptiness of the promise.

We have so few models of men playing the supporting role to their partners. A role Doug Emhoff has fully embraced it seems. We need to normalize men being caregivers and women being breadwinners. This is not rocket science. These are intentional policy decisions that recognize the value of motherhood and equality. Countries that have strong maternity/paternity leave policies and affordable day care options have a much higher workforce participation for women. For parental leave to be most effective in rebalancing the scales it should spilt between both partners. This normalizes the father in the role of caregiver from the get-go. He can build confidence in his abilities as a father and build a strong relationship with his child from the outset. We can create new role models and empower and encourage men to integrate and embody their Yin energies of softness, nurturing, and stillness.

And by doing so we can free them from the shackles of toxic masculinity so they can evolve and reach their own spiritual maturity.

WHEN MONEY CLOUDS MORALS

It is difficult to get a man to understand something,
when his salary depends on his not understanding it.
—Upton Sinclair

One man who stopped lying could
bring down a tyranny.
—Aleksandr Solzhenitsyn

YEARS BEFORE GRETA THUNBERG, I REMEMBER SEEING 12-year-old Severn Suzuki speak at the United Nations Earth Summit in 1992. She was there to urge delegates to take action on environmental issues. She started off by saying she is fighting for her future and has no hidden agenda. She told of how she and her dad used to go fishing in Vancouver until they found the fish full of cancers due to the chemicals that were legally dumped in the water. She talked about being afraid to go out in the sun because of holes in the ozone or breathe the air full chemicals. Then, pointedly to the delegates, "you don't know how to bring back an animal now extinct. And you can't bring back forests that once grew where there is now desert. If you don't know how to fix it, please stop breaking it."

Kids are always so clear on right and wrong. They call us out on our contradictions and half measures all the time. Obviously, the delegates were all kids once. They too knew the right answers. I wonder at what point we bury what we know in our gut, in service to something else? Where is the tipping point when the obvious right actions become clouded with other interests, or the hidden agendas Severn was referring to? And what kind of system requires us to overlook what is so obviously right and in our collective best interests? When is the inflection point where money becomes the driver of all decisions?

The delegates listened patiently as Severn spoke, even though they knew full well nothing she said would influence the outcome of a vote or add teeth to their resolution. They had to get through this bit of theatre to justify upholding the status quo.

Almost thirty years after that UN Earth Summit, Greta has replaced Severn as the face of the future generations. The issues are still the same and the answers are as clear today and they were then. But the same system equals the same result.

I'm not sure when moral clarity become so rare, but I have faith the younger generation will right our path. My daughter become a vegetarian a couple of years ago. I was proud of her, yet at the same time not thrilled at the inconvenience of having to cook two meals at dinner. My son is a full-fledged carnivore. Audrey didn't care about the inconvenience, she cared about the animals. Her priorities were clear. And every time she makes a decision which aligns with her values, her next decision becomes easier too. Of course, the opposite is true. Once you make a decision for the wrong reason, you pull yourself out of alignment. Unless you recalibrate, the next decision will be coming from that unaligned place and soon you will be so far removed from your truth, you'll be Ted Cruz.

What if we all made the next right decision based on our values? Not based on economics, politics or convenience. I know people will stay that's impossible, there are economic considerations or fill in the blank. Well, those economic considerations only exist because of previous decisions we made on what to prioritize. This was not a natural evolution. We made it so. We can unwind these entanglements and realign our systems with our true values. It will be disruptive, but what's the alternative? Doubling down on a system that's already crumbling?

TRUST YOURSELF

There is a voice that doesn't use words. Listen.
—Rumi

Instinct is something that transcends knowledge.
—Nikola Tesla

AN AMERICAN ROBIN MADE A NEST IN OUR WINDOWSILL at the top of my stairs. I see it every time I go to my bedroom. There are three blue eggs in the nest and the mother spends most of the day sitting on them. She changes her position occasionally, but otherwise is still. For several days I have watched this tiny bird, calm in her knowing, patiently waiting for her eggs to hatch. Sitting alone just inches from the path of predators (three humans and a dog) she does what she came here to do. She's alert but not distracted by anything around her.

When I was pregnant, I bought the bible, "What to Expect When You're Expecting," along with several other books. I was advised to make a birthing plan. My brain wanted to control nature, because that's what I've been taught. That felt safe. Nature had other ideas. Anderson's birth looked nothing like my plan. It ended with an emergency C-section after fourteen hours of labor and failed forceps. Sigh.

That didn't dissuade me from getting even more books after the birth by "experts" on breastfeeding, sleep training, bonding. All very natural events that apparently have become so unnatural there are thousands of books written on these topics. I was so used to looking outside myself for answers I didn't trust myself to navigate some of the most natural and instinctive acts a women can experience. So rather than sit still in my knowing, I remained detached from my instincts and devoured the information in the books. With every chapter I read, the less confident I felt. Now, as I sit looking at the robin, I understand the cost of separating myself from my instincts. For the robin that would surely mean death. For me, it was a sort of living death. A separation of my mind from my body and spirit as years of programming taught me to do.

DON'T EQUATE EDUCATION
WITH WISDOM

We've bought into the idea that education is about training and "success," defined monetarily, rather than learning to think critically and challenge. We should not forget that the true purpose of education is to make minds, not careers. A culture that does not grasp the vital interplay between morality and power, which mistakes management techniques for wisdom, which fails to understand that the measure of a civilization is its compassion, not its speed or ability to consume, condemns, itself to death.
—Chris Hedges

WHEN I WAS LOOKING AT SCHOOLS FOR MY KIDS, WHO were in kindergarten and grade 1 at the time, I wanted one that nurtured their creativity as much as their brain. Because I believe if you disconnect from your creativity you disconnect from your innate knowing, your life force. That's why authoritarian governments repress artists, poets, writers, singers, and all form of self-expression. If you're not free, it's very hard to create.

I took tours of several private schools in Toronto.

They terrified me. It seemed to me, they were developing prototypes, not people. They talked about coding and entrepreneurship, developing leaders and innovators. They used words like rigor, foremost, and elite.

"One hundred percent of the kids receive university offers" one school's website claimed, one third of them in science. Let's examine that for a second. So out of one hundred kids who graduated last year, all of them choose to apply for university? How can one hundred freethinking individuals all choose the exact same route—university. How does opportunity look the same for 100 percent of the kids? That's not freedom, that's a system. That's programming to a certain end. Are these schools truly creating "outside the box" leaders or teaching kids how to become employees?

WOMEN ERASED

You can't be what you can't see.
—Marian Wright Edelman

A mistake repeated more than once is a decision.
—Paulo Coelho

Do you know Cecilia Payne? Nor did I until a few months ago. Dr. Payne was an astronomer and astrophysicist who discovered the elements that composed the universe. Her discovery profoundly altered how we look at the stars, sun, and planets. And according to the current Dean of Science at Harvard, her work should be considered as profound as Darwin or Newton's. While a student at Harvard she wrote what was called "undoubtedly the most brilliant PhD thesis ever written in astronomy." Though, in 1920 Harvard wouldn't award PhDs to women so Radcliffe College bestowed it instead.

Several years ago, National Geographic put together a list of "forgotten" women scientists who discovered among other things, the structure of DNA (Rosalind Franklin), nuclear fission (Lise Meitner), and disproving the quantum mechanics law of parity (Chien-Shiung

Wu). None of these brilliant women were credited for their work. Instead, their male colleagues received all the recognition and awards.

This got me thinking about a tour of a boys school in Toronto I took in 2019. As part of this tour, myself and other prospective parents, were taken to the library. The glass display cases at the front contained about fifty books. All of them written by male authors. I seemed to be the only one who noticed.

I don't think it's a stretch to draw a direct line from Cecilia Payne, Rosaline Franklin, Lise Meitner, Chien-Shiung Wu, and so many other women being left out of our history books, and the state of that library display case in a prestigious boys school in Toronto.

All of these omissions required conscious decisions or complete obliviousness.

At the end of the tour, I asked the Headmaster how boys, being schooled only with other boys, were supposed to understand the female experience if they aren't even encouraged to read books by female authors? We know male authors have a male protagonist over 80 percent of the time, and the most common adjective used to describe a female in a book written by a male is "pretty."

I have a white boy. In his day-to-day life, he rarely comes up against friction. He walks through the world as if it was made for him. Because it was. He doesn't really have to contemplate the female condition (though I try to make sure he does). He can go about his day unaffected by the hurdles and barriers "others" encounter multiple times a day. So, to find a "progressive" school perpetuating inequality by not giving the female experience or voice equal prominence in its library reinforced how much work there is to do. Women, minorities, and LGBTQ don't get the "luxury" of not understanding the white male experience. As much as these minority groups need to hear their stories told, white boys and men need to hear these same stories. It's time white men honor, appreciate, and understand the BIPOC, female, and LGBTQ experience as deeply as these groups understand white men.

TRADITION IS THINLY
VEILED PATRIARCHY

> *These mountains that you are carrying,*
> *you were only supposed to climb.*
> —Najwa Zebian

> *You many not control all the events that happen to*
> *you, but you can decide not to be reduced by them.*
> —Maya Angelou

I EVENTUALLY CHOOSE A COED SCHOOL FOR MY KIDS. MY daughter's uniform was a dress shirt, skirt, and knee-high socks. At the end of the day the kids were dismissed onto the playing field. Audrey used to play soccer with the other kids until I arrived. Then one day she stopped. She became self conscious because sometimes when she ran her skirt would lift. And she was at the age when the boys would tease that they saw her underwear. Of course, she was wearing shorts under her skirt, but that didn't matter.

I asked the school why the girls had to wear skirts. It seemed to me the policy was just reinforcing gender stereotypes and the roots were in a tradition that no longer serves us, or more correctly, never served us.

Why should girls be required to wear something that's uncomfortable, impractical, and restricts how they move, and in some cases, what they participate in? Not only that, but they must walk the halls several times each day worrying whether a boy will flip up their skirts. The very thing we make them wear each and every day to school, makes them feel a sense of vulnerability. It requires them to be constantly on guard and vigilant. And in turn we, inadvertently or not, make them normalize that feeling. No wonder it's hard for girls and women to say, this doesn't feel right. This isn't OK. Because they've been taught that this is just the way it is. Girls endure, tolerate, accept. Stay small.

CHOOSE YOUR VALUES OR
THEY WILL CHOOSE YOU

*The things that matter most must never be at
the mercy of the things that matter least.*
—Johann Wolfgang von Goethe

*In the end, these things matter most. How
well did you love? How fully did you
live? How deeply did you let go?*
—Buddha

WE MOVED TO BALI IN 2019 FOR NUMEROUS REASONS, BUT
a big part was to break out of the mind-numbing routine
of a system that didn't value the things I value. Things
like community, creativity, and freedom.

When we started at the Green School in Bali, the
days were entirely different. So much so that my kids
complained they weren't learning anything. I argued that
learning about a different culture, working in the rice
patties or participating in ceremonies was learning. But at
nine- and ten-years-old they had already bought into the
programming of their old school system that prioritized
a very narrow range of subjects – math, science, business.

At such a young age they were convinced that their system was the one right way. Not only had they accepted the boxes that they were put in, but they were asking to remain in them.

I held firm as I didn't want my kids sitting at a desk for six hours a day being fed information so they could pass a standardized test. I don't see the value in uniformity. Humanity is a big mosaic. We all have our own place and part to play and it's hard to find what lights us up when everything around is asking us to conform. The value is in differences of perspectives and experiences. And when the time comes, if my kids choose to apply for university and the admissions people don't feel the same way, then that's not a school I want teaching them.

A few weeks in, Audrey's Green School class was presenting at the school assembly. They choose to make a mandala on the auditorium floor. She and her classmates gathered in the middle of the room and each child carefully placed their flower petals, leaves, or rocks they had gathered. It took ten or fifteen minutes. No words were spoken. No explanation was needed. Just kids, in the moment, creating something beautiful. When they were finished, we enjoyed it in silence for several minutes before it was swept up to make room for something new.

What an amazing lesson on impermanence and change. What if all kids learned at a young age about letting go? Would we fear death in the same way? Or would we embrace it as the natural cycle of things? Would we try to control the uncontrollable or would we embrace flow? These seemingly small lessons are really the big life lessons. They are what ultimately result in a quality of life that is not quantifiable by a salary or job title, but by peace of mind, contentment, and freedom.

I realized early on, most schools teach the opposite of mindfulness. Kids arrive at school usually confident in who they are and what they want. Their intuition is strong. Then we train it out of them with rules and structure. We teach them to override intuition with logical thinking, thus separating the mind from the body and spirit. Tragically our kids must give up parts of themselves in order to succeed in the current education system.

MEDIA IS NOT NEUTRAL

Tyranny is the deliberate removal of nuance.
—Albert Maysles

I worked in television news for six years. I did some writing, producing, and very occasionally, reporting. I never liked being on camera as I felt like a fraud. I was uncomfortable reporting on a story I was given just eight hours before. I met so many viewers who took everything they heard on a newscast at face value and assumed reporters were experts, or at least really well versed, on what they were reporting. The truth was, because of budget cuts, "beats" were mostly a thing of the past. Back in the heyday of journalism, reporters used to be assigned a "beat"— City Hall, transit, the Courts. They had a chance to really get to know their subjects and subject matter. When I was working in the newsroom, we were pretty much all generalists. I got a story at 10 a.m. and had until 6 p.m. to research the topic, find "experts" to interview, then write a script before heading to the edit booth to package it. Because of the time restraints, we usually went to the same few experts over and over. They knew the drill, came prepared with a soundbite and that made things simple. Unfortunately, it also meant a very narrow range of voices were heard and diversity of opinion did not really exist. Of course, experts are people, and they have biases and blind spots and, depending on who they work for, political considerations.

As a reporter on a deadline, I didn't have the time or sufficient background to mitigate that risk. I could google to verify facts and data, but once something is on the web it becomes truth— whether it's true or not. And the repetition of that fact reinforces it.

Adding to my discomfort, news stories used to be two or three minutes long. But they were soon cut to a minute and a half after management received a report by a consulting firm concluding that's the average viewers attention span per story. This meant complex issues had to be simplified to such a basic level they become almost meaningless. Expert's clips became five second sound bites. No context or depth could be conveyed in that amount of time. And much of what is necessary to make an informed decision is left out.

We see the result of this dumbing down in our everyday discourse around almost every issue. We only have patience for clean, tidy narratives. Therefore, complex topics are reduced to right or wrong, good or bad, with no room for anything in between. We are forced to pick a side, to judge everything rather than recognizing there are sometimes conflicting truths depending on your perspective.

We don't watch the news in our house, except around election time. In 2020 CNN and MSNBC were on for approximately eight hours over the course of the US election. During that time my kids started to parrot what the anchors and pundits were saying about Donald Trump. Then they started to mock him with a tone of moral superiority, because that's what they heard on tv. This terrified me. I may not agree with most of what Trump says, but over the course of a few days I watched my kids become polarized and discount everything Trump said based on what others said about him. I admit, I wanted my kids to see the absurdity in Trump. But not because someone else told them to, because they used discernment. The end doesn't justify the means, which ultimately was a form of mind control.

ALL THE ANSWERS ARE IN YOU

I searched for God and found only myself. I
searched for myself and found only God.
—Rumi

WHEN I WAS YOUNG MY MOM TOOK US TO CHURCH EVERY Sunday. We got dressed in our best clothes and sat dutifully in the pews for the hymns and sermon. Church never resonated with me, there were too many inconsistencies, and my queries were more often than not met with unsatisfactory answers. Church was something I did once a week for an hour. It had no relevance in my life the rest of the week. The disconnect made me feel highly uncomfortable every time I entered the building.

When I was in my late teens I stopped going. I started reading spiritual books in my early twenties. I knew there had to be more to life than what I had been told up until that point. I was surprised to find that most teachings of the metaphysical masters have a common message at the root, which was essentially: love one another, we are all interconnected, and God/spirit/the creator (whatever you choose to call it) is inside you.

73

That fact that God wasn't something I needed to obey or worship, but rather was something I needed to uncover internally, felt right to me. It also felt empowering. When spirit and matter are one, humans live in harmony with the natural world. We access the good within us. We don't need laws to tell us how to behave.

But of course, when humans created religion around these teachings, they placed God outside of us. They created convoluted rules and dogma. They created habits, robes, and dress codes. They made us go though priests, pastors, and popes to have access to God. They said if we don't follow the rules, we will be punished. Humans put spiritually in a box for their own purposes. "God" did not. And in human's limited ability to conceptualize "God" they devised a man in the sky who was judgmental and punitive. As if the power that created this mysterious and miraculous planet would be as small-minded and dysfunctional as a human. Human's version of God was to be feared, because we know fearful people are easier to control.

THE BUSINESS OF MEDICINE

The money's in the treatment, not the cure.
—Bret Weinstein

FOR SEVERAL YEARS AFTER PAUL DIED, I WAS NUMB, SAD, and despite sleeping ten hours per night, had zero energy. I had talked to a therapist and felt like I had worked through the trauma of Paul's sudden death and all the stuff that came afterwards. I couldn't understand why I wasn't feeling better. I was otherwise healthy. If I had gone to my doctor, I know she would have prescribed antidepressants. But I didn't want to take drugs to make me feel better. Clearly my body was trying to tell me something and I wanted to understand the root of my unhappiness— not mask it with pills.

One day I listened to a podcast where the author Michael Pollan spoke about his book on psychedelics "How to Change Your Mind." For the book, Pollan researched a variety of plant medicines and psychedelics and discovered firsthand their ability to heal. Research has confirmed the profound benefits psychedelics can have on depression, anxiety, PTSD, and addiction. These outcomes were known and widely studied in the 1960s by some of North America's top universities.

Then the Nixon government, facing resistance from "hippies" to the Vietnam War and simultaneously trying to suppress the Civil Rights Movement, declared a war on drugs. As one of Nixon's top aides admitted, "We understood that we couldn't make it illegal to be young or poor or black in the United States, but we could criminalize their common pleasure." As I said earlier, if there are corrupt individuals, there are corrupt systems. And so, politics simultaneously co-opted the medical system, the educational system, and the criminal justice system.

Marijuana, psilocybin (magic mushrooms), and peyote (cactus) were classed by the FDA, a supposedly independent body, along with heroin as schedule 1 drugs. Schedule 1 drugs are considered to have no medical benefits and are highly addictive. Of course, in the case of the former three, this was provably false and the "experts" at the FDA knew it, but our systems do not operate independent of each other. So, through pressure and eventually policy, the values of the dominant political party were imposed on supposedly independent systems.

These natural plants, that have been used for centuries by native cultures worldwide for sacred ceremonies, were declared more dangerous and addictive than cocaine and meth. University research was halted. And the government succeeded in separating not only the "hippies" but the native Americans and Mexican Americans from their traditional medicines. But at the same time said, here, take ours— alcohol, nicotine, go to town. These are "safe" drugs. Pharmaceutical drugs full of synthetic chemicals made by "scientists"— safe. But not the plants that hold the wisdom of the creator.

What started as Nixon's war on peace-loving hippies and the Civil Rights Movement, has resulted in more people in US prisons for drug offenses than any other "crime." When these laws were passed, if someone was caught with one gram of crack, they would receive a sentence one hundred times longer than someone with one gram of powder cocaine. Of course, it's the same drug, but crack is perceived to be used mostly by blacks and powder cocaine by whites. The gap in sentencing has lessened over the years but it's still massive. The racial bias continues in the opioid crisis. Opioids are primarily seen as a white drug and therefore commonly treated by law enforcement as an addiction issue, not a criminal offense.

But let me get back to mushrooms. After listening to Pollan, and then doing my own research, I was convinced this was the path to take. I found a guide in Toronto and took a trip deep into my unconscious. Over six hours I watched my life unfold in front of me as if I was looking down from 30,000 feet. I saw two things that happened before the age of ten that dramatically altered my life. Both events I remembered as an adult and neutralized them as nonevents. I had no idea the effect they had on my life.

No amount of talk therapy would have uncovered this. The mushrooms removed my ego so I could access my unconscious. My ego has been trying to keep me "safe" my entire life. Its job is to make up stories to save face, to control situations, and to align circumstances with

77

beliefs. Or, in other words, to distort reality. My ego was in the way of seeing myself and the world clearly.

When I was five, I was with my dad at a construction site. There was an open fire and he told me not to go near it and then walked away to check on something. I beelined for the flames. When he saw me he yelled at me to back away. I was horrified and ashamed. When we returned home, I was sent to my room. I sat there stewing in shame and embarrassment. As a five-year-old I didn't understand that my dad was only trying to protect me. Of course, he had a very natural reaction to me standing too close to a fire, but it caused a wound. And the wound started a pattern because of the story I then told myself. My five-year-old self decided I never wanted to be singled out and embarrassed like that again. So, to protect me, my ego devised a plan to keep me safe, which meant making sure I never had to feel that way again. Always vigilant for threats, my ego made sure I never took risks, broke rules, or didn't do anything other than what (I thought) was expected of me. That resulted in 40 years of keeping myself small for fear of failure or judgment or doing it wrong.

The second incident happened on the playground at school when I was around ten. One day my group of friends decided they no longer wanted me as part of their gang. It was devastating. I told myself that I wasn't worthy of love, that I didn't do "it" right. And then and there I decided never to fully trust anyone again. And since then, I have been careful to never get too close to anyone. In my adult years I became hyperindependent. That was a trauma response. I thought if I didn't reveal myself fully,

I couldn't really be rejected. And that pattern ensured I never fully connected with anyone.

For decades I was controlled by these old wounds. They dictated how I moved through the world, how I behaved, responded, and related to others. And I had absolutely no idea.

For the rest of the session and the entire second session, I lay in a fetal position, crying and purging the forty plus years of negative emotions lodged in my body that I never before let myself feel. There were layers and layers of disappointment, heartbreak, loneliness, anger, fear, and frustration that I needed to free from every cell in my body.

I thought I had as close to perfect of a childhood as anyone. But I realized everyone has wounds, no matter how idyllic their childhood. Trauma isn't always a major event; the seemingly smallest slight can cause a wound that creates a story and then a pattern.

WHO AM I?

It's not forgetting that heals. It's remembering.
—Amy Greene

Healing does not mean the damage never existed.
It means the damage no longer controls our lives.
—Akshay Dubey

TO BE CLEAR, THE MUSHROOMS DIDN'T HEAL ME, BUT THEY gave me a roadmap to recovery. I saw myself clearly for the first time. Prior to taking them, I had no idea what my blocks were. I actually had no idea I had any. I thought my numbness was related to Paul dying but I learned the numbness started years before, when I started piling on all the layers of who I thought I should be in order to feel safe and fit in.

After the mushrooms, the question became, was who was I without the stories I told myself, the belief systems and the layers and layers of protection I created?

It was the start of a self discovery and healing path that couldn't be bypassed. It become clear I had to heal myself, so I didn't perpetuate the trauma or pass it on to my kids. I had to unpack the stories I told myself and

81

the stories society told me that I accepted knowingly or unknowingly throughout the years.

I was blessed to meet Nicole, a wonderful intuitive guide in Bali. She taught me how to access my feelings, to look at my shadows and stories and free myself from their bondage. We set about dissolving my "false selves" by unraveling all my belief systems, recognizing my triggers, and subsequent modes of behavior. I began to understand myself in a new way. Being vulnerable is the scariest thing I have ever done, but it was the only way I could learn to connect with myself and from there connect authentically with others.

YOU CAN HEAL YOURSELF

You find answers when you remove what's useless.
—Maxime Lacace

The source of most diseases is in the spirit.
Therefore, the spirit can cure most diseases.
—Nikola Tesla

In Whistler I met Eve, an energy worker who helped me continue to clear the stored emotions in my body. Emotions are energy and if you block them or push them down, like most of us are taught to do, they get stored in your cells, organs, and tissues. This wreaks all kind of havoc. My body was warning me for many years, initially with small aches and pains, lethargy, and eventually more urgent signals, like my hair falling out.

Emotions exist to give you information about a situation. We are meant to feel them then let them move through our body. If we resist them, they stay around longer, and if we ignore them and push them down, they get stuck and cause pain and disease.

This awareness needs to be at the forefront of treatment for any health issue. Talk therapy on its own doesn't work as it does not recognize the mind, body, spirit connection. Pills on their own are Band-Aids and don't get to the root of the issue. Healing needs to come on all levels, or it is only temporary.

Our medical system is built on flawed beliefs or incomplete information. And the known or accepted ways of treating people keep us from finding a better way— healthier, less toxic way. Like thoughts for instance. You've heard of the placebo effect. That's just a thought. "I will take this pill and it will make me better." And often it does. Contemplate the implications of that.

Because the medical system can't understand or explain that effect, let alone patent it, they discount it. But just because we don't fully understand something yet, it doesn't make it less true.

The traditional medical system will tell you your genes dictate your future health. But epigenetics will tell you the genes that are expressed based on our individual level of consciousness and therefore our reactions and interactions to our environment. We have much more control over our health then we've been led to believe.

Don't get me wrong, this is not a call to disregard experts. This is a call for discernment. No one is more of an expert on your body than you. If a practitioner or treatment doesn't resonate with you, find one that does. Take back your power and trust yourself.

THE FUTILITY OF WAR

If we don't transform our pain we transmit it.
—Richard Rohr

THIS MIGHT SEEM IRONIC, BUT THE US MILITARY IS NOW funding millions of dollars of psilocybin research as a treatment for PTSD. They are faced with skyrocketing disability payments, as over 40 percent of soldiers who served after 9/11 have a "service-connected disability."

So just to recap, the Vietnam War stopped psilocybin research and it took another war in Afghanistan and Iraq to eventually restart it.

It is no wonder there are such high rates of mental illness in soldiers. In basic training they break cadets like they would a horse. They remove all traces of their humanity and free will. They separate the soldiers mind from their body and spirit. Then they build them back as machines.

In "An Intimate History of Killing," Joanna Bourke explains how recruits she studied initially resisted killing. To create more efficient killers, the military had to find ways to overcome this. For instance, its desensitization training now uses human forms rather that bull's-eye targets. It has created hyperrealistic weapon training scenarios so soldiers learn to kill reflexively.

After active duty, veterans then return to their suburban homes and are expected to live a normal life. How exactly does that work? We broke them and now we expect them to unbreak themselves? Is it any wonder many turn to drugs or alcohol to numb?

America has been at war in Afghanistan for over twenty years with nothing to show for it. The country is no safer. War begets war. War is an energy, and we are lobbing that energy back and forth.

What if America used the US$2.2 trillion it has spent on the war to develop clean, renewable energy sources? Then America would never need to set foot in the Middle East again.

TOXIC TECH

None of the most powerful tech companies answer to what's best for people, only to what's best for them.
—Tristan Harris

Magicians start by looking for blind spots, edges, vulnerabilities and limits of people's perception, so they can influence what people do without them even realizing it. Once you know how to push people's buttons, you can play them like a piano.
—Tristan Harris

VIDEO GAMES, SOCIAL MEDIA, AND SELFIES ARE THE BANE of my existence. All three numb or distract us. And you can overlook a lot of things when you are numb and distracted. Maybe that's the point?

As a parent, willful blindness can equal sanity at times. Giving your child that extra hour of screen time can mean finishing that Zoom call in peace or some much needed alone time. How much longer are we willing to ignore what we know to be true and at what cost?

Rates of teen depression in the United States shot up 60 percent between 2009–2018. Over 36 percent of teens report having persistent feeling of sadness or hopelessness. And 18.8 percent had seriously considered suicide. Why aren't we mobilizing to address this the way we did for COVID-19?

It's normal to want to believe the best. That companies wouldn't knowingly create a product that is highly addictive, modifies our behavior, influences our habits, and collect all types of information on us. Except we know better. Frances Haugen, the brave Facebook whistleblower only confirmed what we knew in our hearts to be true.

Former Silicon Valley developers have been sounding the alarm for years now. One former Google developer, Tristan Harris, says the iPhone is so addictive it's like a "slot machine in my pocket." These devises are designed to maximize the amount of time we spend on them. Sure we can exert our willpower to limit our use but there are "thousands of people on the other side of the screen whose job is to break down whatever responsibility I can maintain" continues Harris. If adults can't get a handle on this, and let's be honest, we can't— I'm guilty of bringing the phone from room to room in my home in case, God forbid, I don't get a text the second it's received. I'm even guilty of occasionally checking my phone in the bathroom.

Social media is a whole other beast. Kids aren't interacting with their friends, they are creating and reinforcing false selves. With few exceptions, every time they post a picture, click like, or upload a video they are distancing themselves from their true selves. Sure, we can say "it's how they communicate these days," but unless communication has become comparing yourself to others or constantly seeking external validation, I call bullshit.

Navigating these platforms are treacherous, and no one escapes unscathed. And we expect kids to manage this land mine.

We wouldn't give our kids cocaine, but we have no problem handing them an iPad. Brain scans show the effects are similar. And we know that to be true because we've all had the experience of asking our child twenty times to turn off the iPad and then having to physically pull it out of their hands. We don't recognize the behavior that comes after that. The normally reasonable child becomes a tyrant.

Big Tech won't help us. It has every reason not to. Nor will the government. Let's take back our power and act on what we know in our gut to be true.

OWNING OUR POWER

We talk about how many women were raped last year, not about how many men raped women ... this passive voice has a political effect. It shifts the focus off men and boys and onto girls and women ... Even the term "violence against women" is problematic ... It's a bad thing that happens to women ... It just happens. Men aren't even a part of it!
—Jackson Katz, PhD

Reflection and action must never be undertaken independently.
—Paulo Freire

AFTER THOUSANDS OF YEARS, THE FEMININE ENERGY OF the Great Goddess is remerging all around us. Can you feel the shift? It's the power behind the regenerative social movements like Me Too, Black Lives Matter, along with the renewed urgency of environmental action. In Canada we are finally facing the horror of the murders and abuse of over 150,000 Indigenous children at residential schools at the hands of our government and the church. We are rising up against the continued logging of our last remaining old-growth forests. Things that were in front of us all along, we are now choosing to see. We are bringing the dark into the light to be transformed.

The feminine energy is taking back its power, making a full-fledged defense of her life and values while women are simultaneously stepping into our fierceness and wildness. We are exerting our sovereignty and rejecting the one-sided values that have been imposed on us for centuries.

When it comes to Me Too, women are rightfully angry and rageful. We want and deserve a public airing of our grievances. We need those in power to recognize our pain that was born through the injustices of the patriarchal system.

At the same time, we must continue to keep at the forefront that the balance of energies is the goal. We must be careful not to become what we oppose. All women should be heard should not be conflated with all women should be believed.

Truth is the ultimate goal. It must be. We can't right the wrongs of the past by swinging the pendulum too far in the opposite direction. Some debts cannot be repaid.

THE PATH FORWARD

*The best way to keep a prisoner from escaping is
to make sure he never knows he's in prison.*
—Fyodor Dostoevsky

*The secret of change is to focus all of your energy
not on fighting the old, but on building the new.*
—Socrates

I USED TO BELIEVE OUR VALUES WERE FIXED AND INHERITED,
like hair color or blood type. The world was the way it
was and I found a way to move within it. When I used
my voice, it was often to reinforce the status quo. I had
a lot riding on the status quo. My whole life was built
around it. I always sensed its limitations, but rather than
questioning it, I found ways to work within the system to
get things done. While I knew the system was flawed, I
also understood it, found "work arounds," and navigated
it relatively well.

This, my friends, is a trap.

It keeps so many of us women, powerful and not so
powerful, working to uphold a dysfunctional system. The
devil you know. Change is hard. But change is necessary.

The planet's slow death is a mirror of our own deadly systems, structures, and values. We are now seeing very clearly what we created. We can't move forward while holding onto old beliefs, systems, and ways of beings.

We made this world, and we can remake it. There are answers to our problems, but not if we expect to monetize them all. We need to discover who we are without our wounds individually and collectively. Imagine what we can create from our healed, whole selves. What if our systems were designed to uplift and support us, not wear us down and beat us into submission. What if the workplace was structured like a circle, not a ladder? What if societies metric of success was collective well being, not gross domestic product? This is all within our reach.

Discontent with the status quo is at an all-time high and dissenting voices are being amplified due to the power of social media. There has been a shift in generational values, and with the new generations a desire and urgency for change. Today, less than half of millennials support capitalism in its current form. As societal norms and values are shifting, power is shifting along with them. Many are opting out of the traditional workforce. They are saying no thank you to modern day serfdom. And that is good news for anyone seeking structural change.

For the first time in history, we have the technology to mobilize millions of people from seemingly disparate groups to push for a common goal of justice— economic, social, political, and environmental.

The majority of people in Western cultures subscribe to Yin values of cooperation, sustainability, group decision-making and building community. I talked about resonance earlier. And how structures are reinforced by our continual use and the values of those structures are replicated along with them. This is not a passive process, but the wind is at our back every step of the way. We must make conscious choices each day about what we want to reinforce. My decisions will connect to your decisions and millions and million of others and together we will recreate the world.

If you are on the planet today, you are on humanity's hero's journey. Your work is now. Dig below the surface. Question the status quo. Then choose…consciously.

ACKNOWLEDGEMENTS

I could not have written this book without the guidance and mentorship of two very special women. We moved to Bali because of the Green School, but I now know it was really so I would meet Nicole Bridger. Nicole, thank you for creating a safe space for me to crack open. Thank you for pushing me to go deeper, for helping me see clearly, and for empowering me to trust my own internal guidance system.

And Eve Casavant, an energy worker and equine facilitator in Whistler/Squamish. Eve, thank you for helping me tear down my walls, dissolve damaging belief systems, and purge the emotions stored in my body. To all the beautiful horses of Kind Spirit Horses and Cheekye Ranch that partner with Eve, thank you for teaching me to get out of my head, be still, listen, and let go. Your generosity and purity of spirit are transformational.

To Paola Martis, a beautiful and powerful soul living in Bali, thank you for guiding me to write this book and giving me the direction it needed.

To Anderson and Audrey, thank you for teaching me every day about love and living in the moment.

To my parents Sherrin and Tony, thank you for a

lifetime of love and support and for your boundless love for your grandkids. To Julie, Marisa, Chris, Lauren and Natalie, I am so grateful to be on this journey with you.

To my chosen family who inspire, support, and show up for me constantly. Especially to Tim Gamble who has been my biggest supporter for more than twenty years. To the talented Savannah Lockie who created the cover art, thank you for living an authentic life, it is equally inspiring and liberating. To Joanna Rotenberg, for creating my on-ramp back to work and for sharing your first born with us. To Jennifer Burke, who I know I can call at any time of day and you would show up in an instant with food, wine, and great advice. To Jennifer Mackenzie, for years of conversation and always creating space at your table for us. To Gabriela von Pfetten, whose open heart and compassion showed me a new level of connecting. To Allan Holmes, whose door is always open and perspective always refreshing.

And to Daniel Gallucci and Brad White, thank you for putting the pieces together during that fateful week in Hawaii and for your support ever since.